IMAGES OF ENGLAND

NOTTINGHAM
A CENTURY OF CHANGE

A blizzard in 1969 creates a scene of beauty, although the pedestrians and travellers queueing for buses in the Old Market Square would probably have disagreed.

IMAGES OF ENGLAND

NOTTINGHAM
A CENTURY OF CHANGE

DOUGLAS WHITWORTH

The
History
Press

First published in 1997 by Tempus Publishing Limited,
Reprinted 1999, 2004

Reprinted in 2010 by
The History Press
The Mill, Brimscombe Port,
Stroud, Gloucestershire, GL5 2QG
www.thehistorypress.co.uk

ISBN 978 0 7524 0767 8

Typesetting and origination by
Tempus Publishing Limited
Printed and bound in Great Britain by
Marston Book Services Limited, Didcot

To Margaret, with love

The Flying Horse Hotel, The Poultry, 1966. The hostelry, which dates from Elizabethan times, has had a history of rebuilding. The façade was redesigned in 1934 with plasterwork based on the Rose and Crown at Saffron Walden in Essex. In 1967 an application to demolish the inn was refused but in 1987 permission was given for it to be converted into a shopping arcade.

Contents

A familiar sight on Radford Road in 1968. Shipstone's greys, as these horses were known, were used locally long after the need for them had passed. The nearby Star Brewery ceased production in 1991, and finally closed in 1994.

Acknowledgements

I would like to thank Martin Sentance for allowing me to use many of Frank Stevenson's evocative photographs.

I would also like to thank John Lock and Iain Smart for all their help, and the following for the loan of photographs:

Nottingham Post, The Boots Company PLC, Nottingham City Council Leisure and Community Services – Local Studies Library, D.J. Archer, C. Hardy.

My thanks are also due to Dorothy Ritchie and the staff of the Local Studies Library for all their kindness and help.

Introduction

Nottingham acquired the status of a City during Queen Victoria's Diamond Jubilee year. The letter from Lord Salisbury, the Prime Minister, to Edward Fraser, the Mayor of Nottingham, announcing the award is dated 18 June 1897, but it was not until 7 August 1897 that the Charter conferring the dignity of the title of City of Nottingham was signed. A Centenary, especially one occurring towards the end of a millenium, is a time for reflection. This new collection of photographs of Nottingham is a personal review of the scenes and events in the city during that momentous century.

Nottingham is now almost unrecognisable from the smoky town of a century ago. Although the street plan of the city has not altered significantly, Nottingham has changed from a town composed of predominantly Victorian buildings to one with a mixture of architectural styles.

The first major project in the new city was the clearance in 1897 of the area east of Milton Street in preparation for the construction of the Victoria Railway Station. This involved the demolition of many rows of houses and also the Nottingham Union Workhouse in this crowded neighbourhood.

The death of Queen Victoria, coinciding with the beginning of a new century, brought in a new era. The streets of all Britain's large towns and cities were taking on a new appearance with the arrival of motor cars and electric trams. A hundred years ago the industrial scene in Nottingham was dominated by the lace industry, but within twenty years this was to decline through loss of trade due to the First World War and changes in fashion. During this period, however, the famous Nottingham industries, Boots, Players and Raleigh, all of which were founded in the last quarter of the nineteenth century, were expanding rapidly. The widening industrial base, together with the traditional machine knitting companies, gave the city an economic stability which enabled it to prosper during the general depression of the 1920s and '30s.

The first great change of the century occurred in the 1920s, when Friar Lane was widened and the old Exchange was demolished. The cost of the replacement building was a very contentious issue, as was the banishment from the Market Place of both the covered market and Goose Fair. The neo-Classical Council House which replaced the Exchange seemed rather grandiose, but Nottingham people have come to appreciate their impressive town hall.

T. Cecil Howitt, the architect of the Council House, also designed several other distinctive buildings in the city during this period. These include the Woolwich Building Society offices on South Parade and the Raleigh Cycle Company's head office on Radford Boulevard. Apart from the redevelopment of Albert Street, Lister Gate and part of Upper Parliament Street in the 1930s, there were few other planned changes in the city centre until after the Second World War.

The great achievement of the Corporation between the two wars was the clearance of the slum properties of Broad Marsh, Narrow Marsh and Sneinton Bottoms. The inhabitants of these areas were subsequently rehoused in new council estates built mainly in the north and west of the city.

The most important development in education in the 1920s was the building of the University College at Highfields. Sir Jesse Boot bought a large estate at Highfields with a view to building a model factory on the land, but his immediate successors at Boots lost interest in the scheme. When Alderman Edmund Huntsman suggested the site would be ideal for the new

University College, Sir Jesse Boot tackled the project with great enthusiasm and put into it the sum of £500,000. The new college was opened by King George V in 1928, and it was on this occasion that the Mayor of Nottingham was given the style of Lord Mayor.

The Second World War affected the lives of everyone in the country, the threat of enemy air raids having the most impact. Nottingham suffered only one blitz, in May 1941, remembered vividly by all who experienced it. The damage to public and commercial property, although severe, was not on the scale suffered by other cities, and rebuilding by the City Council went ahead without urgency. Nottingham's slum clearance programme, halted in 1939, was not recommenced until 1945, the year in which land for council house building was bought at Clifton. Over one thousand pre-fabricated houses were built in Beechdale and Aspley in the first two post-war years, some of which are still in use. The construction of permanent council houses was also resumed and over 15,000 were built between 1945 and 1965.

In 1946 and 1947 the River Trent overflowed its banks and flooded large areas of the city, particularly the low-lying Meadows. The Trent River Board began an extensive flood defence scheme which included changing the course of the river at Colwick.

In 1949 Nottingham celebrated the Quincentenary of the granting by Henry VI of the Great Charter which made Nottingham a county in its own right. These celebrations had more impact in Nottingham than the Festival of Britain, held in 1951, which was designed to lift the spirits of the nation after the austerity of the 1940s.

The 1950s saw the building of Clifton Bridge to relieve the bottleneck of traffic at Trent Bridge. The decade also saw the beginning of the construction of Maid Marian Way. This involved cutting across numerous old streets with the loss of many fine properties, notably the Collin's Almshouses and St Nicholas' Rectory. The planned Inner Ring Motorway, which would have cut across the corner of the General Cemetery and part of the Arboretum, was fortunately rejected by the government in 1970.

During the 1960s no overall building plan was followed and the face of Nottingham suffered from the rash of piecemeal developments. With the exception of its clock tower, the Victoria Railway Station was demolished in 1967 following the closure of the line during Dr Beeching's rationalisation of the railways. The Victoria Shopping Centre was built on the site, and at the same time a similar shopping centre was constructed in Broad Marsh. The building of the latter centre sadly entailed the demolition of Drury Hill, one of the oldest streets in Nottingham. Since the building of these two shopping centres the City Council has pursued a policy of conservation, which has prevented the mistakes of the past being repeated. Parts of the city have been pedestrianized; although creating traffic problems elsewhere, this has enhanced the quality of the environment in the main shopping area.

The opening in 1982 of the Royal Concert Hall saw the end of a saga extending over thirty years. This fine hall now attracts audiences from the whole region and beyond. New life is being brought into the area adjoining the Nottingham Canal. The Inland Revenue Centre and the Magistrates Courts are both architecturally invigorating and are part of a scheme which includes new offices, hotels and leisure facilities.

At the beginning of the twenty-first century the city has been transformed again with the introduction of a light rapid- transit system, a multi-purpose ice arena on the site of the old ice stadium and a redesigned Old Market Square.

The improvement of the amenities in Nottingham in recent years, together with the influx of other races, has changed the city from being merely provincial to cosmopolitan.

The first hundred years of the City of Nottingham have passed, and now this vital and prosperous city has entered a new century as the undisputed capital of the East Midlands.

One

Edwardian Nottingham

The decorations in Chapel Bar for the Diamond Jubilee of Queen Victoria in 1897. Although the majority of the population of this country had never seen her, the Queen was more popular than she had ever been. The Diamond Jubilee celebrations, held on the Forest in June 1897, were watched by vast crowds. The announcement during the celebrations, by the mayor, of the elevation of the borough to city status gave great satisfaction.

The Market Place in 1900, when almost all road traffic was horse-drawn. The man dressed as a minstrel is carrying a billboard on his back advertising the Livermore Court Minstrels who were due to appear at the forthcoming Goose Fair.

Long Row and Market Street in 1912. Griffin & Spalding's department store, in the centre, is in a prime position; this Victorian building remained here until 1926 when it was rebuilt. On the left, under the statue of Queen Victoria, are the pot stallholders with their wares laid out on the pavement.

Ice cream vendors next to the statue of Queen Victoria, c. 1908. The two Italian families of Solari and Capocci were well known in the city, and each rose from being stallholders to the ownership of well-established businesses. Brigida Capocci, who is standing behind the second stall, was also a fortune-teller, and after coming to England in the 1880s she tramped the country with a barrel organ before settling in Nottingham.

The Exchange in 1906, with an open-top bus at its city terminus; these buses had just been introduced onto the streets of Nottingham. With solid tyres, they were an uncomfortable form of transport. The entrance to the Shambles, the open butchers' stalls which were to remain for another twenty years, is on the right.

A butcher at work in primitive conditions in the Shambles in 1919. This is the stall of Alfred Truman. Together with the other butchers, he moved to the West End Meat Market on Long Row West when the Exchange was demolished in 1927.

An open-top tram on the Sherwood route turning into Long Row from King Street in 1905. Electric trams appeared on the city streets in 1901, and a year later the Corporation discontinued its horse bus services, some of which were taken over by John Cummings, a private operator.

Sneinton Market, c. 1915. In the background are the Victoria Buildings, opened in 1877 as a municipal workmen's dwelling block. In 1988 the City Council sold the block, now named Park View Court and in need of modernization, to a private company. After refurbishment, new life was brought into this important piece of Victorian town planning.

Sir John Rees, the Unionist candidate for East Nottingham, speaking from a carriage at an election meeting outside J. Howitt & Sons' printing works in Ashforth Street in 1912. The by-election was won by Sir John with a majority of 1,324, but the result was overshadowed by the news of the sinking of the *Titanic* a day earlier.

Opposite: An election rally in Alfred Street Central in 1912. The rally was addressed by Sir John Rees, the Unionist candidate for the East Nottingham parliamentary constituency. Everyone in the crowd, almost without exception, is wearing a hat, those of the ladies being large and eye-catching.

South Sherwood Street in 1896. The buildings on the left were soon to be demolished and replaced by the Empire Palace of Varieties. Thomas Forman's newspaper office, from the balcony of which election results were announced, is on the right. An ice-cream seller is taking a rest beside a cast-iron public convenience, with two children for company.

Cab drivers waiting for fares in Waverley Street on a wet day in 1914. The horse and cabby on the left are both wearing capes: the men, at least, could take refuge in the shelter to the right of the picture.

Harry Read standing by his horse and cart in 1903. He served Boots for fifty-one years, eventually transferring to motor transport. His son Vincent carried on the family tradition, working in Boots transport department for fifty years.

Several types of delivery vehicles outside Boots General Offices in Station Street, c. 1910. The first lorry is electric-powered, the next four vehicles being three- or four-wheel petrol-driven models.

Skating on the frozen River Trent in 1895, the last occasion when this was possible. The winter of 1895 was one of the coldest of the nineteenth century and many rivers were frozen over. Crowds were attracted to Trent Bridge, not only to skate but also to watch the spectacle.

The steamer *Empress*, by Turney's Quay, *c.* 1910. This boat, together with the *Queen* and the *Sunbeam*, were pleasure craft owned by boat-builder A.J. Witty. Trips were made between Trent Bridge and Colwick Park, where entertainment and refreshments were provided. The *Empress* was sunk in 1940 whilst on its second crossing to Dunkirk during the evacuation of troops from France.

Two

The Nineteen Twenties

Children and adults enjoying the simple pleasure of a see-saw in 1924.

Dorothy Vernon's house in Friar Lane in 1921, then one of the few links with the Middle Ages remaining in Nottingham. Dorothy Vernon and her husband John Manners lived here for six years after their elopement from Haddon Hall in 1572. When this building was demolished in 1927 Nottingham lost one of its few remaining features of architectural, historical and romantic interest; it incorporated the only surviving remains of the Carmelite Friary which had previously been on this site.

Mrs Darby, on the right, having a gossip with one of her neighbours in the Abel Collin's Almshouses in 1926. These were splendid looking dwellings, but they had stone floors and poor facilities. When Maid Marian Way was planned to pass nearby in the 1950s, the City Council, to its discredit, ordered their demolition.

Opposite: A view over the chimneys from Nottingham Castle in 1923. The church with the square tower is St Nicholas, which was rebuilt in 1671-8 after the earlier church had been demolished on the orders of Colonel John Hutchinson at the end of the Civil War. The spire of High Pavement Unitarian Chapel partly hides the fifteenth-century parish church of St Mary.

21

A seventeenth-century house at the corner of St Nicholas Street in 1922. This street was called Jew Lane in the thirteenth century, after the number of Jews living in a ghetto in this part of the Norman borough. Following the banishment of the Jews from the country in 1290, the street took the name of the nearby church.

An eighteenth-century school on Short Hill in 1922. Mrs Kate Burrows, the occupant of this building, was one of many in the lace finishing trade in this area. The steep hill from High Pavement leads to Short Stairs, one of the ancient routes from the old town to the Meadows.

Drury Hill in 1923, probably Nottingham's most photogenic and certainly most lamented street. This medieval street did not fit into the plans for the Broad Marsh Centre in the late 1960s, and the thoroughfare is now only a memory.

A university carnival float advertising Boots products in 1925. The annual rag organised by students in aid of local charities was a popular event in the 1920s and '30s.

A Napier van, one of Boots extensive fleet of vehicles, in the early 1920s. This van has a range of accessories fitted to the exterior, including an acetylene headlamp, oil side lamps, bulb horn and an illuminated sign.

A row of Boots lorries with their bonnets raised, at a show in the 1920s. Boots were regular exhibitors at agricultural and county shows, displaying not only their range of vehicles and products but also their pedigree cattle.

A trolley bus at the junction of King Street and Queen Street in 1929. Trolley buses were first used in Nottingham in 1927, but this was the first type to have the inflatable tyres which made for a smoother ride.

The construction of the Council House in 1927. The foundation stone was laid on 17 March of that year and progress was rapid. However, the market stalls remained in the Market Place until November 1928, when the Central Market in King Edward Street opened. The statue of Queen Victoria, in the foreground, was removed to the Memorial Gardens on the Victoria Embankment in 1953. Near the statue are Italian ice-cream sellers and the Enterprise Refreshment Stall, which advertises 'Tea the great reviver'. Round the island at the bottom of Market Street is an assortment of transport including trams, an open-staircase bus, and motor cars.

The Council House in 1929, the year it was opened by the Prince of Wales. Although the building was criticised for its mixture of architectural styles, it has now become a much-loved feature of Nottingham.

A group of figures representing 'Civic Law', one of the four groups of statues at the corners of the dome of the Council House. This group was sculpted by Charles Doman, a prize-winning student of the Nottingham School of Art.

Boys from the Nottingham Gordon Memorial Home, playing on the land behind the home in Cranmer Street in the 1920s. The Gordon Boys Home, as it was usually called, was founded in 1885 as a home for destitute boys and was originally situated in Shakespeare Street. In 1904 a new home for the charity was opened in Cranmer Street, where it remained for over fifty years before moving to Alexandra Park. The need for this sort of charity decreased, and in 1965 the home was closed.

Boys and one girl dressed for a pageant at the Lenton Junior School on Empire Day, 24 May 1929. These children represent the countries of the British Empire and are obviously taking their roles seriously.

Three

The Nineteen Thirties

William Hollins' Viyella House decorated for the Coronation of King George VI in May 1937. This office and warehouse, with its striking design, was opened in 1933 and was a great advertisement for the company. As a Grade II listed building, it was fortunately saved from demolition in 1984 and subsequently refurbished.

Barges on the Nottingham Canal in 1930. Traffic on canals was predominantly commercial in the years between the two world wars; the Trent Navigation Company owned this warehouse and others on Meadow Lane, Trent Lane and at Colwick. This building has been renovated as part of the redevelopment of the area, including the building of a footbridge over the canal.

Two water-skiers skimming over the water near Trent Bridge in 1939.

Opposite: The Victoria Embankment in the 1930s. A quiet day for Brookhouse's, whose pleasure boats sailed to both Wilford and Colwick. Nottingham people come here to promenade along the river bank or just to sit on the embankment steps.

The demolition of Red Lion Street in 1933. The slum dwellings of Broad Marsh and Narrow Marsh were finally being pulled down, although it was to be another forty years before the whole area was redeveloped. Mary Collins' shop on the right remains open, but with a dwindling number of customers.

Workmen bricking up some of the caves uncovered during the demolition of the back-to-back houses in Red Lion Street in 1933.

Condemned properties in St John Street, *c.* 1933. Lower Parliament Street, which until then ended at Broad Street, was being extended to Carter Gate. Gelsthorpe's newsagents shop, established in 1845, has a chalked sign pointing to its new premises on the line of the new road. A surveyor on the right is measuring levels, and a model T Ford lorry owned by Whitmore's, builders of Hucknall Road, is in the centre.

A famous shop in Goose Gate in 1934. After the death of her husband John in 1860, Mary Boot and her son Jesse, opened a herbalist's shop here at 38 Goose Gate. Jesse gradually took over more control of the business, and in Kelly's Directory for 1876 the shop was listed as Jesse Boot, Herbalist. Six years later he leased 16-20 Goose Gate for 100 years and then began rebuilding the premises which, when completed a year later, became his first fully-equipped chemist's shop.

Boots Beeston site in 1938, the year the D.6 building in the foreground was opened. The D.10 factory in the centre, which, like the D.6 building, was designed by Sir Owen Williams, was opened in 1933 and is now a Grade I listed building. Jesse Boot's dream was to build model factories surrounded by houses like those at Bournville and Port Sunlight, but he died before the completion of his vision.

The spectacular glass architecture of Boots D.10 building – like a modern Crystal Palace. The factory was designed to provide ideal working conditions and was immediately hailed as a 'wonder factory'.

Girls working on packing lines in Boots D.10 factory, known familiarly as the 'Wets', in 1938. The impression is one of unhurried speed.

Boots High Street store in 1933. This imposing shop, built in 1903, was the model for many other Boots department stores. As well as selling a great range of goods, the shop had a café and a Booklovers Library. This shop closed in 1972 when Boots opened their branch in the Victoria Shopping Centre.

The tram and bus depot in Manvers Street in 1936, the year trams ceased to run in Nottingham. As well as trams due to be scrapped, there are several types of trolley bus – or 'trackless' as they were colloquially called.

Buses parked by Holy Trinity Church in Trinity Square in 1930. The first bus is an AEC Regent 3, the first 'modern' type double-deck bus operated by the City Transport Department. The public house in the background is the Dog and Gun, which was demolished in 1958.

A trolley bus passing the Walter Fountain at the junction of Carrington Street and Greyfriar Gate on a winter's day in 1939. This is now the location of the Lister Gate entrance to the Broad Marsh Shopping Centre. The Walter Fountain was built in 1866 in memory of John Walter MP, the chief proprietor of *The Times*, by his son. It was demolished in 1950.

The Collin's Almshouses in Carrington Street in 1930. These almshouses and those built in Friar Lane were established through a charity founded by Abel Collin. Both sets of almshouses have now been demolished, these in Carrington Street in 1954 after standing empty for sixteen years.

A row of eighteenth-century cottages on Kennel Hill, previously known as Chimney Hill, off Mansfield Road, in 1932.

Four

The Nineteen Forties

Boots factory girls in a concrete air raid shelter in 1940. This looks as if it may have been a practice, but all have their gas masks with them – this was a habit which gradually fell into disuse.

The bomb-damaged University College on Shakespeare Street after the blitz of 8/9 May 1941. The Registry Office, the Moot Hall, St John's and St Christopher's Churches were among the other important buildings which were destroyed. This was the worst air raid on Nottingham during the Second World War, though the city suffered ten other raids which caused a total of 181 deaths.

A Boots fire team in Island Street in 1940. Together with the City Fire Brigade and the Auxiliary Fire Service, they were severely tested on the night of the blitz when nearly 100 fires were started. The Boots printing works on Station Street were completely burnt out and the Nottingham Co-operative bakery in Meadow Lane was also hit and forty-nine people killed.

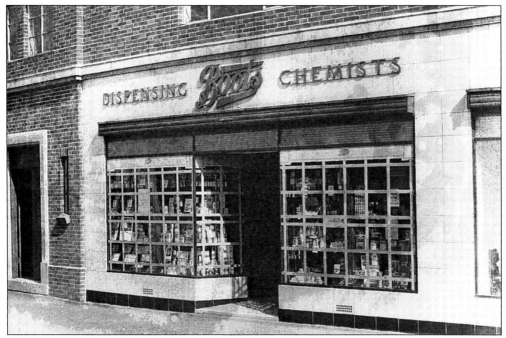

Boots the Chemists shop on Thackerays Lane in 1940. The tape stuck on the window was a precautionary measure against bomb blast. Among the products in the shop window were 100 Aspirins for 9d. Saccharin tablets and medical kits are also well displayed.

The crowd in the Old Market Square at 3 p.m. on VE Day, 8 May 1945, when Mr Churchill was broadcasting to the nation. This was the day for which the whole population had been working and waiting, and it was one of great emotion.

Upper Parliament Street in 1944. Having dug a hole in the road, workmen are talking in a group and two policemen and a serviceman stand watching. The two women turning into Clumber Street are dressed in the fashion of the day and the two girls approaching are members of the Air Training Corps.

The Old Corner Pin public house at the junction of Upper Parliament Street and Clumber Street on a wet day in 1949. This eighteenth-century inn was originally known as the George, later became the Horse and Groom, and by 1912 it had been renamed the Old Corner Pin.

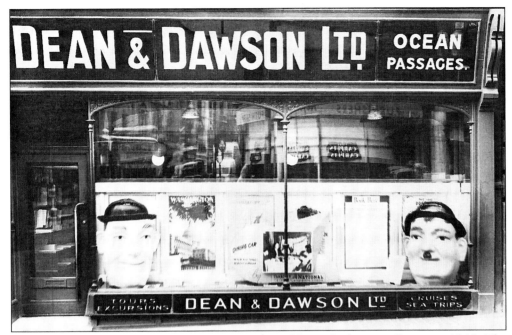

The window display of Dean & Dawson Ltd on Upper Parliament Street in 1946. The promotional material in the window relates to a tour of this country then being made by Laurel and Hardy. Thomas Cook & Son, Sanderson's Express and Dean & Dawson Ltd were the only travel agents in the city at a time when foreign holidays were a rarity for the majority of the general public.

Theatre Square from Wollaton Street in 1949. The Gaumont cinema, until 1948 known as the Hippodrome, on the left, was to remain open until 1971. The County Hotel, with its curved façade, was demolished in 1976 when it was found to be unsuitable for incorporation in the scheme for the renovation of the Theatre Royal.

The Victorian atmosphere of the Nottingham Mechanics Institution reading room in 1945. There are old prints on the walls, desks for newspapers, and requests for silence. The Mechanics Institution then had a library, a billiard room, a tea-room, whist and chess clubs, and was home to several societies.

Bromley House Library reading room in 1949. Formally known as the Nottingham Subscription Library, it has been housed in Bromley House, Angel Row, since 1821. The house dates from 1752 and has several rooms of architectural merit. At the rear of the house is one of the few remaining private gardens in the city centre.

Deer in Wollaton Park find grazing difficult in freezing conditions in 1947. The park was transformed by the snow and the many slopes became toboggan runs for both adults and children.

An unusual phenomenon in the abandoned Sherwood railway tunnel in 1947. Icicles hanging from the roof made a striking picture in the grim winter of that year.

Men and boys clearing snow from the Nottingham Forest football ground in 1947. This was a winter of severe weather conditions; freezing temperatures in January and February were followed by heavy rainfall in March and widespread flooding. The 1946/47 football season was extended into June because of the accumulation of postponed matches.

Floods at Trent Bridge in March 1947. With the sudden thaw and heavy rain, one eighth of the city was flooded, the worst affected area being the Meadows. After these floods the Trent River Board decided to take action and a flood defence scheme was undertaken.

Boots employees being transported by lorry through the floods in 1947. The low-lying Boots site at Beeston was liable to flooding in severe conditions and workers had to walk along duckboards to reach the factories and offices.

A train running through flood water at Basford Crossing in 1947 makes a dramatic picture. The River Leen overflowed its banks in 1946 and 1947 causing serious flooding in the surrounding streets and houses.

Steam locomotives in a grimy Victoria Station in 1946. Locomotives sending clouds of smoke and steam into the air still hold a fascination for many.

The broken wall of the Lower Parliament Street railway bridge gives this young boy a bird's-eye view of the trains steaming below.

Fred Stone, in the right foreground, haranguing his audience in the Old Market Square in 1948. He was known as the Slab Square Bible Thumper; he held no brief for the orthodox church and would revile his listeners. Aged 88, he had been preaching in the Square for over fifty years. The young man in the raincoat, facing the camera, is John Peck; he later became the Communist councillor for Bulwell East and then a Green Party councillor for the same ward. On the left are several Mormons listening attentively.

Folk dancing in the Old Market Square during the Quincentenary celebrations in 1949. These commemorated the 500th anniversary of the granting, by Henry VI, of the Great Charter to Nottingham. This made the town a county in its own right and changed the status of the bailiffs into sheriffs.

Not a scene from *Gulliver's Travels* but a girl retouching a 10ft by 7ft photograph, the largest ever made in Nottingham up to that date. The photograph, printed by Marshall & Company, was exhibited at the Trades Exhibition in Broad Marsh during the Quincentenary in 1949.

Princess Elizabeth and the Duke of Edinburgh arriving at the Victoria Railway Station for the Quincentenary celebrations in June 1949. After the war years and the continuing austerity, the Quincentenary gave the citizens of Nottingham a chance to celebrate. Many events were held throughout the city, including pageants, a water carnival, exhibitions and concerts. To mark the event the Nottingham Co-operative Society commissioned Alan Bush to compose a Nottingham Symphony which was performed at two of the concerts given at the Albert Hall.

Council houses in Beechdale Estate in 1947. Several hundred of these aluminium pre-fabricated houses were erected in Beechdale and Aspley in the years immediately following the Second World War. Although they were intended to be only temporary dwellings, many of them have now been modernized and are still occupied.

The Council House dominating the city in 1948. In the foreground are several Georgian houses, and Copestake, Crampton's lace factory is prominent in the centre of the photograph.

Five

The Nineteen Fifties

A family enjoying the sunshine in the Memorial Gardens on the Victoria Embankment in the 1950s. The gardens were the gift of Sir Jesse Boot, who made the announcement of his offer in his acceptance speech when he received the Freedom of the City of Nottingham in 1920.

The construction of the new embankment on the south bank of the River Trent in 1952. After the disastrous floods of 1947 the Trent River Board began the flood defence scheme which included dredging and widening this stretch of the river.

North Wilford in 1956. On the left is the gatehouse of the Wilford Toll Bridge, known locally as the 'Ha'penny Bridge' from the toll made for pedestrians. The bridge was closed to cars in 1974 as it was unsafe, and rebuilt in 1982 when it was re-opened for pedestrians and cyclists only. Beyond are the chimneys of the North Wilford Power Station, which was opened in 1925 and continued producing electricity for the Nottingham area until it was closed in 1981. On the right is Clifton Colliery which, together with the Wilford Toll Bridge, was opened in 1870. In 1943 this colliery was the first pit in the country to be nationalised; it was to remain open until 1969.

Opposite: Boys fishing in the River Trent at Wilford in 1955. Warm water from the nearby power station drew fish to this stretch of the river and encouraged the anglers. On the far bank is the fourteenth century church of St Wilfrid.

An outing on the River Trent for members of a local club on a summer afternoon in 1955.

The *Pride of the Yare* steamer on the River Trent in 1959. Beyond the crowded pleasure boat, where the elm trees of Lovers' Walk once stood, preparations are being made for the Nottingham Regatta.

Crowds watching the Nottingham Regatta in 1959. The embankment steps make a perfect grandstand for the thousands of people attending the regatta in scorching weather. The entertainment included speed boat races, a circus, donkey rides, fireworks and illuminations.

Arkwright Street, near Atlas Street, in 1959. Most of the buildings in Arkwright Street were architecturally undistinguished but this corner house was an exception. Parked by the kerb are two old-style window cleaner's barrows – without a window cleaner in sight!

Workmen clearing the garden of the Collin's Almshouses on Carrington Street in 1951. After the closure of these almshouses in 1938 the building was purchased by the Co-operative Wholesale Society as the site for a proposed eight-storey emporium, but the war prevented this development. In 1954 the City Council bought and demolished the derelict buildings.

A Nottingham Co-operative Society delivery van passing the corner of Muskham Street and Bunbury Street in 1959. This district, together with St Ann's, was redeveloped in the 1970s when entire streets of property were demolished and new terrace houses were built. The Plumtre Arms, later the Plumtree Arms, is now the only building in this photograph which remains, although converted into flats. A new school and playground now occupy the land in the background.

Temporary huts in Broad Marsh in the 1950s. This wasteland was used for various events in the 1940s, such as exhibitions and fairs, but in 1952 a bus station was opened here. In the background is the prominent steeple of the High Pavement Unitarian Chapel and beneath it is the old High Pavement School.

The balcony of the Scala Cinema in Market Street in the 1950s. The Scala was opened as the Alexandra Skating Rink in 1875, but in 1876 the building was converted into the Talbot Palace of Varieties. After a short spell as the Gaiety Palace, the music hall became Nottingham's first picture house, known as the King's Theatre. In 1913 the cinema was renamed the Scala, finally becoming the Classic in 1967 before closing in 1979.

A busker playing a trumpet and an accordion for an audience of children in a Nottingham back street in the 1950s. One little girl seems unimpressed and has turned her back on the musician.

Troopers of the Household Cavalry giving drill instruction to cub scouts in Wollaton Park during the Festival of Britain in 1951. The trooper of the Blues and Royals, on the left, shows a cub scout how a sword should be handled, whilst a trooper of the Life Guards gives advice to the other boy.

A troop of the Royal Army Service Corps leaving the Low Level Railway Station on London Road in 1952. They were on their way to Wollaton Park to participate in the Bath and West Show being held there. The officers are wearing black armbands in mourning for the late King George VI. The Corporation Eastcroft gas works are in the background, one of three such plants in the city at this time.

Lenton Lodge in the 1950s. Built in 1823, this was originally the entrance gate to Wollaton Park. After the sale of Wollaton Hall and Park to the Corporation in 1924, part of the land was resold for housing development and the lodge left completely isolated from the hall. The canal near the lodge was closed in 1936 and later filled in.

The Council House and the Old Market Square illuminated for the Coronation of Queen Elizabeth II in June 1953. All the towns and cities of the country vied with each other to present the best display of flags and banners.

The preliminary attraction to the Wild West Show at the Goose Fair in 1959. This type of show, with its sharp-shooting, knife-throwing, rope tricks, and Indian tortures, is no longer seen at the Goose Fair. State-of-the-art fast riding machines now predominate.

Young girls enjoying a ride on a roundabout at the Goose Fair on the Forest in 1959.

The Meteorite ride at the Goose Fair in 1959. The riding machines become more terrifying every year; this one was advertised as 'the sensation of the age'.

The end of the Goose Fair in 1959. Families are watching the fair being dismantled and boys are picking over the debris in search of coins and anything else of value.

The footplate crew and members of the Railway Correspondence and Travel Society before an excursion from the Midland Railway Station in 1955. The viaduct carrying the old Great Central line is in the background.

Members of the RCTS admiring a sight which was then familiar enough, but still had power to thrill. This class B12/3 No. 61554 engine, from the Eastern Region of British Railways, was a redesign by Nigel Gresley of an earlier Great Eastern locomotive.

Holidaymakers boarding a train at the Midland Railway Station in 1957. This was a non-corridor carriage and comfort was at a premium, but once a seat had been gained – by a window for preference – the holiday had commenced.

An aerial view of Holy Trinity Church and the Victoria Railway Station in 1952. The future of both the church and the station appeared secure, but in 1958 the church was demolished and replaced by a car park. In 1967 the demolition of the railway station began, although the clock tower was left standing, to be replaced by the Victoria Shopping Centre. The offices and printing works of the *Nottingham Evening Post*, in the centre foreground, have now been replaced by the Cornerhouse, an entertainment complex, and production of the newspaper has been transferred to new premises in Canal Street.

Lower Parliament Street in 1959. On the left is the former entrance arch to St Stephen's Church, all that remained after the church was pulled down in 1897. Above it is a figure of a horse, advertising the shoeing forge which occupied the premises for some years. The small hut beyond is the south entrance to the Victoria Railway Station – for ticket holders only.

Derby Road in the 1950s. The Albert Hotel, on the right, survived an explosion in 1911, but in 1970 it suffered the fate which overtook other respected buildings in that decade – demolition. On the near corner is Stuart Smalley's hatter's shop, another Nottingham institution.

Trinity Square in 1953, five years before these buildings were demolished. On the corner is Will Hill, bespoke tailor, this being an age in which men invariably wore suits. In front of the Army Recruiting Office is an army pick-up, an electric milk float and a Rover 75 car.

The Newton Building of the Nottingham and District Technical College in 1959, the year after it was officially opened by Princess Alexandra. In the background is the Nottingham Playhouse, which began life as Pringle's Picture Palace in 1910 and became the Goldsmith Street Picture House in 1913. In 1942 the Repertory Theatre opened here and, after a period during which it was known as the Little Theatre, the Nottingham Playhouse opened in 1948. This theatre closed in 1963 when the newly built Nottingham Playhouse opened in Wellington Circus.

The Nottingham and District Technical College from the air in 1959. The college has now expanded over the whole of the surrounding area, requiring the demolition of complete rows of houses. In 1992 the college achieved university status and is now the Nottingham Trent University.

Automobile Association patrolmen help a woman driver who has skidded onto the grass verge at Clifton in 1955.

A car being towed through flood water by an AA patrol vehicle on Wilford Lane in 1955.

Six

The Nineteen Sixties

Broad Marsh bus station in the 1960s. Although it has the appearance of being temporary, the bus station remained here from 1952 to 1968. The last houses in Broad Marsh were then pulled down and the building of the Broad Marsh Shopping Centre began.

Carrington Street in 1960. The extension to the Woolworth store which replaced older property, is on the right.

Nottingham Castle from Collin Street in 1961. The car park which replaced the Collin's Almshouses remained until the Broad Marsh Shopping Centre was built. Paddock Street, in the centre, has on it the premises of E. Watmough & Company, the well-known confectioners, and behind is the structure of the new People's College of Further Education.

The junction of Lister Gate, Broad Marsh and Carrington Street, known as 'Lucky Corner', in 1964. Montague Burton's 1920s style shop, built to impress, has a new fascia and logo. The building on the left is now the only one remaining. Although this is probably the shortest street in Nottingham, it still bears the name 'Broad Marsh'.

Roadworks in Carrington Street in 1966. A new road layout making the north end of Carrington Street one-way only was being introduced.

Severn's on Middle Pavement in 1964. The building on the right was part of a merchant's house built around 1450 and was threatened with demolition when the Broad Marsh Shopping Centre was planned. Fortunately, the timber-framed building was saved and re-erected on Castle Road (see p. 102). The Georgian house on the left, with its intricate carving around the door, was unfortunately not saved.

The interior of Severn's Restaurant in 1964. Severn's was an old-established restaurant and coffee house with an adjoining wine and spirit business, and it was sadly missed when it closed.

The wooden structure of Severn's is clearly visible in this 1968 photograph. This was the front part of a much larger house and is one of the oldest examples of domestic architecture in Nottingham.

An atmospheric photograph of a part of Nottingham which has now completely changed. A coal train is passing Weekday Cross signal box in 1960. These steps, the train-spotters' ideal viewpoint, which led to Middle Marsh, disappeared when the Broad Marsh Shopping Centre was built.

The almost-deserted platforms of the Victoria Railway Station in 1960. This typical Frank Stevenson photograph, with its light and shade, shows the fine architecture of the station. The last train left Victoria Station on 2 September 1967, and ten days later the demolition contractors began work.

The Mechanics Cinema just prior to its demolition in 1964. This, the second Mechanics Hall on the site, was opened in 1869 and converted from a lecture hall to a cinema in 1916. The small circular building adjoining the Mechanics Cinema is the Christadelphian Ecclesia.

The demolition of the Mechanics Cinema in 1964, allowing for a short time a clear view of the Victoria Railway Station. After the whole block had been pulled down a new building, named Birkbeck House after the founder of the Mechanics Institution movement, was built and opened in 1966. This has now been replaced by a block of shops.

A worm's-eye view of the footbridge over the Victoria Railway Station in 1969. The clock tower of the railway station appears undamaged from this angle, but over the railings was a scene of destruction as the station was demolished.

A woman and her daughter avoiding a ladder and, hopefully, bad luck, in Forman Street in 1965. The Empire Theatre had been closed for seven years and was never to re-open, being demolished in 1969. The Empire Café on the left was a haven for many theatre-goers.

A panoramic view of the demolition of the Victoria Railway Station in 1968. The station was opened in 1900 and closed in 1967, and during that period it won the affection of many Nottingham people. The clock tower, which remains today, is a reminder of the railway station which many believe should have been saved. In the foreground is the footbridge between

Milton Street and Glasshouse Street, which continued to be used until the construction of the Victoria Shopping Centre. Some of the intricate ironwork of the station is still visible on the left, as are some of the platforms and steps.

The rear entrance to the Black Boy Hotel in 1960, with the dome of the Council House looming in the background. On the right are the offices of the *Nottingham Evening News*, with the newspaper chute attached to the wall. Following the merger of the *Nottingham Journal* with the *Nottingham Guardian* in 1953, the *Nottingham Evening News* amalgamated with the *Nottingham Evening Post* in 1963.

The Black Boy Hotel on Long Row East in 1964. This short stretch of road lost most of its character when the hotel was pulled down in 1970 to be replaced by a modern building. Although established centuries ago as a posting house, the hotel was reconstructed in 1887 by Watson Fothergill, who made further alterations in 1897.

The figure of the black boy which was rescued from the Black Boy Hotel when the building was demolished. The complementary figure of a black girl has still to be traced.

The busy Nottingham city centre in September 1963. North-bound buses are travelling up Queen Street past Watson Fothergill's Queen's Chambers, completed in Queen Victoria's Diamond Jubilee year of 1897.

Exchange Walk during the January sales in 1966. Farmer's drapery store, on the left, was built on the site of Thomas Smith's bank, which in 1658 was the first bank to be established in the provinces.

An old-fashioned cast-iron lamp standard in Exchange Walk. In the distance are the spires of Alfred Waterhouse's Prudential Building at the junction of King Street and Queen Street.

A white-coated and helmeted policeman on point duty in Theatre Square in 1962. This decade saw a considerable increase in traffic on the streets of Nottingham, and traffic jams in the rush hour were frequent. One of the City Council's answers to the problem was to construct Maid Marian Way, which has caused controversy ever since.

Theatre Square from Market Street in 1964. The Theatre Royal was then almost one hundred years old and becoming increasingly uneconomic. Touring opera companies such as Carl Rosa and Sadlers Wells continued to perform wonders in the antiquated auditorium. The adjoining County Hotel, one of Nottingham's oldest established hotels, survived until 1976, when the plans to renovate the Theatre Royal made its demolition inevitable. The Scala Cinema on the left was due for another reincarnation as the News and Cartoon Cinema before it became the Classic Cinema in 1967.

East Circus Street Hall in 1960 just prior to its demolition. This hall, originally called the Scotch Baptist Church, was built in 1860 for £4,000. In 1904 the hall was offered to the Congregationalists, who worshipped here until 1938 when the City Council bought the property. It was then used for a variety of purposes, including concerts, school prize distributions, bazaars and lectures. After the hall was pulled down, the new Nottingham Playhouse was built on this site.

Workmen excavating the old town wall between Park Row and Mount Street in 1964. The wall was revealed when the area was being cleared for the construction of Maid Marian Way. This was the western boundary of the medieval town, entrance being through the gateway at Chapel Bar, which existed until 1743.

The 1960s was largely a decade of demolition in Nottingham. These are the remains of the building at the corner of Park Row and Derby Road; the site became the northern end of Maid Marian Way, then under construction.

The sub-post office in Park Row in 1966. This building was notable for the sixteenth-century traceried windows which were rescued from the Houses of Parliament when it burnt down in 1834. Originally a private residence, it was built on the site of St Peter's Poorhouse.

A hive of activity at the Sneinton Wholesale Market in 1965. Completed in 1938, the market concentrated into that area all the wholesale distributors of fruit, vegetables, flowers, fish and poultry. From the early hours of the morning the market resembled a miniature Covent Garden.

Percy Goring's fruit and vegetable stall at the Sneinton Wholesale Market in 1960. The market remained in Sneinton until 1995, when it was relocated in Meadow Lane.

The Central Market in King Edward
Street in 1960. It was sited here from
1928 to 1972, sufficiently long for
stallholders and shoppers to become
accustomed to it and to resent the
move to the Victoria Shopping Centre.

The Granary Café in Hurt's Yard in
the 1960s. The alleyway is a reminder
of the many similar yards which led
from Long Row to Parliament Street in
the nineteenth century, when the area
was known as the Rookeries.

Crowds spilling onto the roadway on Trent Bridge while making their way to the Nottingham Forest football ground in 1960. This was the year after Nottingham Forest won the FA Cup and crowd attendances at home matches were very high.

The end of a race on the River Trent under a heavy sky in 1964. Umbrellas are in evidence, and the wet embankment steps have not encouraged the spectators to sit and watch.

The illuminated Suspension Bridge over the River Trent in 1960. The bridge was opened in 1906 to carry water pipes and was also designed to be a shorter route over the river for the residents of that part of West Bridgford.

The outsize chiming clock in Yates's Wine Lodge on Long Row in 1965. This clock, although no longer chiming, is one of the curious objets d'art remaining from the hundreds which once filled this Victorian showpiece.

A platform clock being removed from the Low Level Railway Station on London Road in 1965. This station was built in 1857 as the terminus of the Great Northern Railway. After the Victoria Railway Station was completed in 1900, this station was used mainly for goods traffic, finally closing in 1972.

Seven

The Nineteen Seventies and Eighties

If the 1960s was a decade of demolition, the 1970s was a decade of rebuilding. The Theatre Royal was purchased by the City Council in 1969 when it was in danger of closing and in 1977 its restoration was begun. The character of the Victorian theatre has been retained but the auditorium has been remodelled and the antiquated dressing rooms and backstage facilities have all been rebuilt.

The Victoria Centre flats under construction in 1971. For the second time in less than eighty years this area has been cleared and replacing the Victoria Railway Station are these flats and the Victoria Shopping Centre.

The Victoria Centre complex from the junction of Woodborough Road and Mansfield Road in 1971. In the foreground is the Pentecostal Church shortly before its closure. The church was built by the Wesleyan Methodists who occupied it from 1872 to 1939. They were followed by the Christian Scientists, who were in turn succeeded by the Assemblies of God. The church was demolished in 1973 when a road improvement scheme was planned.

An aerial view of the Victoria Centre in 1971. The centre was opened in 1972; with the opening of the Broad Marsh Shopping Centre in the same year, the shopping habits of the citizens of Nottingham were changed irrevocably.

Bottle Lane, one of the oldest streets in Nottingham, in 1977. This street led from the Norman borough to the English borough around St Mary's Church. When the Great Central Railway tunnel was being excavated many caves were discovered and subsequently filled in.

The Lace Centre in Castle Road in 1988. The reconstruction here of Severn's building, which had been removed from Middle Pavement, was the compromise reached when it was threatened with demolition in 1968 (see pp. 78-9).

Two surviving seventeenth-century houses on Upper Parliament Street in 1988. Briddocks, a newsagent established for over a century, was well-known for the range of international newspapers and magazines sold. Kismet, the adjacent Turkish kebab house, was one of the many different ethnic food shops now open in Nottingham.

The red terracotta tower and dome of the Midland Railway Station in 1984, after its recent restoration. Following the opening of the Victoria Railway Station, the Midland Railway Company responded by building this station, which was opened in 1904.

Lambert's factory in Talbot Street in 1987. This factory, with its Italianate style clock tower, was built in 1863 by William and John Lambert for their lace dressing and dyeing business. In 1979 the factory closed but was listed as a Grade II building and remained unoccupied until a development company planned its renovation. During the restoration of the building in 1990, a high wind caused the tower to collapse and an identical clock tower was built to replace it.

The balcony and façade of Yates's Wine Lodge in 1978. This was the site of a medieval inn which, from the sixteenth century, was named the Talbot. In 1872 Edward Cox purchased the inn and commenced its reconstruction. When the doors of the new Talbot were opened in September 1874 hundreds of people were waiting for admission. Inside was a Victorian drinking palace with a gallery and flamboyant decorations – the whole filled with sculptures, bronzes and objets d'art. Yates's Wine Lodges bought the Talbot in 1929, beginning a new era in the history of this popular hostelry.

The Bell Inn pavement café in 1989. Since many of Nottingham's streets have become pedestrian precincts, the pavements have taken on a continental appearance. This stretch of Angel Row contains several historic buildings: the Georgian house in the centre is Bromley House, built in 1752 and since 1821 the home of the Nottingham Subscription Library (see p. 45).

Pearsons' department store on Long Row in 1987. This shop opened in 1889 and closed for the last time in 1989. The new owners of the property discovered the timber frames of two Georgian houses behind the façade, which were then given Grade II listed status. The premises were re-opened as retail shops in 1994 but a fire in 1996 severely damaged the interior of the property (see p. 115).

Pearsons' shop frontage on Upper Parliament Street in 1988. This building, named Empire House, was designed by T. Cecil Howitt in 1933 for A.B. Gibson Ltd, wholesale provision merchants. In 1962 Pearsons bought the property and extended the 1933 façade to give a Parliament Street entrance to their store. When Pearsons closed down in 1989 this building was demolished.

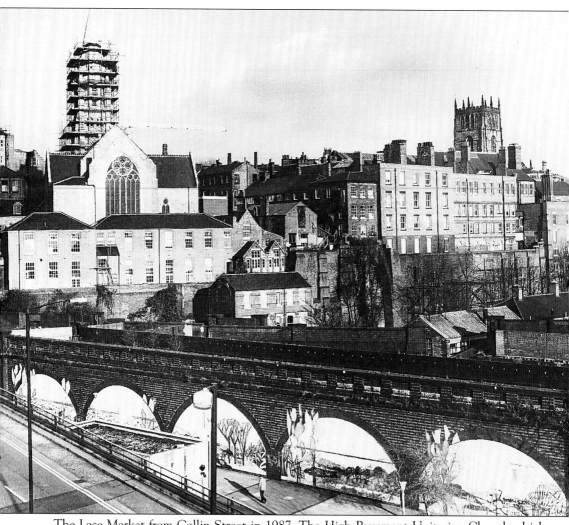

The Lace Market from Collin Street in 1987. The High Pavement Unitarian Chapel, which closed in 1980, is being renovated, including the rebuilding of the spire. The building below the chapel is the old High Pavement School, which opened in 1805 and closed in 1895. In the foreground is the viaduct which carried the Great Central Railway over the Meadows; its arches have been decorated with murals.

The city skyline from Collin Street in 1988. The Unitarian Chapel in the foreground was, in 1988, converted into the Pitcher and Piano, a bar-restaurant, after several years as a museum of lace and an exhibition of working lace machines. Behind the converted chapel are the contrasting architectural styles of the dome of the Council House and the Newton Building of the Trent Polytechnic, now the Nottingham Trent University.

The Jubilee Wing of the General Hospital in 1988. Alfred Waterhouse designed this building which was completed with money from the Saturday Shilling Fund. This fund was established by the mayor to provide a permanent commemoration of Queen Victoria's Diamond Jubilee. This building has now been converted into offices and apartments.

A rare view of the rear of the National Westminster Bank in Thurland Street in 1988. It was possible to take this photograph when the corner block of Pelham Street and Clumber Street was pulled down and rebuilt. The bank was designed by Watson Fothergill in 1882 and has an ornate interior with stained glass windows and a wealth of carving.

Left: Shoppers intent on finding a bargain at Sneinton Market in 1989. The Victoria Leisure Centre in the background was opened in 1896 as the Victoria Baths and included washhouses and laundries. Only the clock tower now remains after the centre has been rebuilt.

Opposite: A stallholder attracting shoppers at Sneinton Market in 1989. In the background is the Ragged School, opened in 1859 and now almost a ruin. Fortunately, this Grade II listed building has been restored by the Nottinghamshire Wildlife Trust, and has become a centre for conservation excellence.

Below: A study in expressions round a confectioner's stall in Sneinton Market in 1989. This stall is well patronised, little encouragement being required from the stallholder.

Shoppers waiting patiently at a haberdashery stall in Sneinton Market in 1989. Since the removal of the nearby wholesale market to Meadow Lane in 1995, this area is being regenerated.

Green's Mill on Belvoir Hill in 1988, following its restoration as a memorial to George Green, the mathematician, who was also the miller here. Born in 1793, he used one of the floors of the mill as a study, and in 1828 published his greatest work, *An Essay on Electricity and Magnetism*, for which he subsequently became famous. The mill was gutted by fire in 1947 but was purchased by a Memorial Fund and presented to the city in 1979.

The birthplace in 1829 of William Booth, the founder of the Salvation Army. This historic house in Notintone Place is now a museum and is incorporated into a Goodwill Centre.

Eight

The Nineteen Nineties

The former Pearsons' building after the fire which virtually destroyed the interior in August
1996. The façade of the property was relatively untouched by the fire and restoration of the
building has now been completed.

The Old Corner Pin at the junction of Upper Parliament Street and Clumber Street shortly after its closure in 1990. This eighteenth-century inn was subsequently rebuilt as a store and lost most of its character (see p. 42). Shoppers are purposefully crossing the street to and from the Victoria Shopping Centre.

Ben Bowers' restaurant at the junction of Derby Road and Wollaton Street in 1996. This distinctive 1877 building was a branch of Boots the Chemists from 1909 to 1964.

Langtrys, at the corner of Forman Street and South Sherwood Street, in 1991. Formerly known as the Peach Tree, it was convenient for patrons of the Theatre Royal and the Empire Theatre. This public house and the many other bars and discos around Theatre Square now attract the youth of the city, particularly at the weekends.

The frontage of Yates's Wine Lodge in 1996, with a new conservatory bar on the first floor (see p. 106). Inside, the Grade II listed building, with its ornate gallery and cubicles, is pure Victoriana. In the years since it was opened as the Talbot in 1874, many of the unusual items which filled the tavern have disappeared but some of the bronze statues and ornaments remain.

A diner with only pigeons for company in the Old Market Square in 1992. On Long Row is one of many fast-food outlets in the city. The adjoining amusement arcade occupies the building opened in 1912 as the Long Row Picture House. The cinema closed in 1930, when J. Lyons & Company opened a tearoom here.

The steps of the new Weekday Cross being used for *al fresco* meals in 1996. This was the site of the old weekday market which continued here until 1800. The old Weekday Cross was demolished in 1804. On the parapet of the railway tunnel in the background are old advertisements for first-class London shows every evening at the Theatre Royal.

A Pakistani food shop in Sneinton Boulevard in 1992. With the influx of many different nationalities into the city, the food outlets have become increasingly diverse. The sign over the shop gives an English translation of the Urdu.

A refreshment stall at the Goose Fair in 1992. These stalls serving traditional Goose Fair food, such as hot dogs and baked potatoes, also provide meals for fairground workers during the construction of the fair.

Workmen erecting a children's roundabout at the Goose Fair in 1993. In three days, dozens of riding machines and stalls mushroom on the Forest site, built mostly by manpower.

The Ranger ride at the Goose Fair in 1996. This is the modern version of the swing-boat, which was fairly sedate in comparison with this machine! In the background is another breathtaking ride.

Girls sketching during the erection of the Goose Fair in 1993. The fair, which for the last century has been essentially a funfair, is now an integral part of Nottingham's year. The view and the noise outside the fair generate an excitement almost as great as that within.

An Asian family enjoying the thrills of the Goose Fair in 1996.

The glass-mirrored entrance to the Royal Concert Hall reflects the *Nottingham Evening Post* building in 1996. The concert hall had been on the drawing-boards since the end of the Second World War but construction work finally began in 1979.

The Theatre Royal in 1996. The theatre is now part of the Royal Centre and is a credit to Nottingham. The imposing portico, which has suffered many changes over the past hundred years, has been restored to its former design. The ugly sign on the attic has gone and the urns which had disappeared have been replaced (see p. 91). The *Nottingham Evening Post* building in the background has been demolished and replaced by the Cornerhouse, an entertainment complex.

The demolition of Boots Island Street warehouses in 1996. Jesse Boot began manufacturing in this area when he rented three rooms in Elliott's lace factory in the 1880s, and by 1892 he had taken over the whole factory. The buildings being pulled down were his first purpose-built factories, completed in 1914.

John Lock and Iain Smart surveying the demolition of Boots Island Street warehouses. John Lock, on the left, together with Colin Marshall, established Boots Museum, and they, like many other Nottingham people, have fond memories of the Island Street warehouses. Iain Smart is the site manager for E.C. Harris, the project management company.

Nearing the end for two Nottingham landmarks. Boots warehouses in Island Street being gutted and, below them, the remains of the High Level Railway Station before its demolition.

A 200-ton girder bridge spanning the Nottingham Canal being lowered to the ground before its demolition. This is one of the bridges which carried the Great Northern Railway and the London Road High Level Station. A 1,000-ton Krupps' crane is lifting this great feat of Victorian engineering.

The Inland Revenue Centre from the Castle in 1996. These distinctive buildings were opened in 1995 and have brought new life to this area. In the left foreground is Newcastle House, which was originally Viyella House. This Art Deco building has recently been restored and an important part of the city's architectural heritage preserved.

The Magistrates Courts beside the Nottingham Canal in 1996. This building was opened in 1995 and was the largest civic project in Nottingham since the building of the Council House. The long-neglected surrounding area is now being redeveloped into an office and leisure complex.

The former General Hospital and chapel in 1996. Until the demolition of the Trent Wing of the hospital in 1994, this chapel, which was designed by T.C. Hine, was hidden from view. The hospital buildings are now the administrative offices of the Nottingham Health Authority.

The dome of the Council House from the Newton Building of the Nottingham Trent University in 1996. From this viewpoint the Council House of this great city still dominates the skyline, with contrasting spires and roofs in close proximity. Nottingham's first century as a city has passed and this vital regional capital of the East Midlands has now entered a new Millenium.